HASTA KALĀ

RADHA BAHL

notionpress.com

INDIA • SINGAPORE • MALAYSIA

ISBN 979-8-90540-963-9

Hasta - hand

Kalã - art

Every tradition in this book began where you are right now — with a hand, a surface and the urge to make something.

To those curious enough to trace the stories hidden in every motif, this book is for you.

Author's Foreword

When I was younger, I was drawn to creating works of art without thinking too much about 'how' or 'why'. I liked repeating shapes, filling in spaces, and letting patterns slowly take form, even if I didn't fully understand what I was creating.

Over time, I realised that these ways of creating artwork were already connected to practices around us, shaped by different cultures, materials, and the glorious traditions of India.

However, I never had something that allowed me to explore that freely on my own terms. This book seeks to fill that gap.

***Hasta Kalā* brings together patterns and forms inspired by traditional Indian folk art, but keeps them open enough to be reimagined.**

It is less about getting things right and more about noticing, experimenting, and continuing the legacy of India's known and established folk art forms.

If I had something like this growing up, it would have been a springboard for my creativity, without limiting what I could do with it.

With *Hasta Kalā*, my sincere hope is that it finds its way into the hands of more young artists who will not only colour these pages but also connect with the stories, traditions, and creative spirit that make Indian folk art so magical.

RADHA BAHL

CONTENTS

WARLI ART | A Language of Circles and Lines

Warli is a tribal art form which originated in the state of Maharashtra. It uses simple shapes like circles, triangles, and lines to show daily life, nature, and celebrations.

Origin

Warli is traced to the Warli tribe in the Sahyadri mountains, which run across Maharashtra and parts of Gujarat.

Materials

Traditionally painted on mud walls using:

- White rice paste
- Bamboo sticks
- Brown mud background

Only ONE paint colour: White
Traditionally painted by women
The tarpa dance is the most famous design

Where is it used?

- Traditional: weddings, festivals, harvest, community rituals
- Contemporary: clothes, home décor, bags, murals in schools, cafés, offices

What makes it special?

- Uses limited shapes but tells detailed stories
- Focuses on nature and community
- An easy-to-recognise minimal style
- No faces; hence, it represents community and not individuals.

Common Depictions

- Farming and Hunting: ploughing, harvesting, gathering food
- Dance: especially, the Tarpa Dance, showing unity
- Rituals: Devachowk, the sacred square
- Marriage: Lagnachauk with the bride and groom
- Nature: animals, birds, forests
- Village life: festivals, cooking, working, music

THE LANGUAGE OF WARLI ART

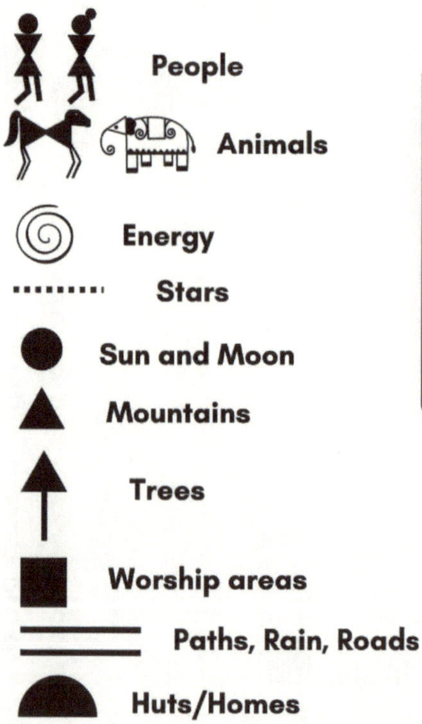

This Warli artwork shows a village scene using simple shapes. The people, made from triangles and circles, are depicted as moving and celebrating together, reflecting community life. Lines and circles form a cart, showing travel and daily work. Trees and plants, made from triangles and lines, represent nature. Birds show harmony with the environment, and the hut, made with a semi-circle and lines, represents home. Overall, the artwork tells a story of everyday village life using simple symbols.

Now it's your turn to tell a Story

Describe your day in Warli art

Self-Portrait in Warli

Favourite Season of the Year

5 things you can't live without

Dream Pet

Where you want to live when you grow up

What do YOU think is happening in this Warli depiction?

Madhubani Art | Walls that once held stories

Madhubani art, also called Mithila painting, has its roots in the Mithila region of Bihar, India. Traditionally, women painted the walls and floors of their homes to commemorate religious ceremonies, marriages, and significant social occasions.

As a result, the art form is closely associated with ritualistic activities and domestic life. Madhubani art eventually spread from building surfaces to paper, fabric, and canvas, preserving the tradition's unique symbolic iconography, bold contours, intricate patterns, and flat use of colour.

What are Madhubani Paintings used for?

- Used in rituals to pray to gods and goddesses
- Painted to celebrate marriages, births, festivals, and seasons
- Believed to bring good luck, protection, and happiness to homes
- Today, it is seen in books, murals, textiles, and framed artworks

> ***Because they are thought to bring wealth and good fortune, fish are frequently used as symbols in Madhubani art.***

Did you notice? Madhubani paintings usually have no empty space in the background.

Instead of using brushes, traditional Madhubani painters painted with their fingers, twigs, or fabric using natural colours.

Motifs and their Meanings

Fish are a symbol of prosperity, fertility, and good fortune.

The peacock is a symbol of elegance, beauty, and love.

A tree represents nature, growth, and life.

The sun and moon symbolise time, equilibrium, and the life cycle.

THINK LIKE AN ARTIST

- Madhubani emphasises patterns just as much as images.
- Lines and dots
- Cross-hatching
- Leaf and floral designs
- Repetition in geometry
- Pattern Fillers

Now YOU become the Artist!

Illustrate your favourite childhood memory in the Madhubani style using the 3 blank strips below. Define the setting. Who's there? What's happening? Add strong outlines, patterns, symbols, and fill in the strips.

Bring this Madhubani artwork to life by colouring it in with bright, traditional colours!

GOND ART | Life in Pattern

The Gond art form can be traced to the Gond tribal group in Madhya Pradesh. With its roots in central India, the art form is typically made on walls, floors, and domestic surfaces to convey narratives, ideologies, and a strong bond with the natural world.

However, Gond art can also be created on canvas and paper. The style's flowing lines, repetitive dots, and intricate patterns used to represent animals, trees, and folklore make it identifiable even when the surface changes.

What stories does Gond Art tell?

- Tales about animals and how they relate to people.
- Legends and folktales that are passed down through generations.
- Well-known religious tales or myths.
- Tales that portray rivers, trees, and forests as sacred.
- Daily activities in the community, such as farming, hunting, and festivities.
- Imaginary and mythical tales featuring animals that resemble dreams.
- Tales of peace, preservation, and reverence for the natural world.

In Gond art, animals are often drawn larger than humans. This is done on purpose to show respect for nature and to highlight the belief that animals, trees, and forests are powerful and important protectors of life.

THE WORLD OF GOND ART

- Animals and birds as important figures, especially fish
- Trees, plants, and forests
- People living alongside nature
- Stories from daily life and folk tales
- Imaginary and dream-like scenes
- Repeated patterns covering the shapes

Patterns make the picture; dots and lines are used to create shapes instead of shading. Patterns fill the forms as they are drawn. This makes the artwork feel active and full of life.

LET'S SEE WHAT YOU IMAGINE!

Draw your dream pet: Use only dots and lines to build the shape and texture, creating a repetitive pattern. This animal doesn't need to be a real one; it could be fantastical! And don't forget to give it a name.

NAME:____________________

TANJORE PAINTING | Sacred and Ornate

Tanjore painting is a traditional Indian painting style that looks vibrant and resplendent. It is known for its bright colours, raised surfaces, and the use of gold foil. These paintings usually depict gods and goddesses and are designed to inspire awe and spiritual wonder.

Origin

Tanjore paintings can be traced to Thanjavur, Tamil Nadu, many years ago. It developed in temples and royal courts, where artists created paintings to show devotion and respect for gods.

Where is Tanjore used today?

Traditionally, Tanjore paintings were kept in homes and temples and used for prayer and worship. People believed these paintings brought peace and blessings. Today, Tanjore paintings are mostly used as framed artworks, religious decorations, and gifts for special occasions.

SOMETHING RARE: Tanjore paintings are meant to catch attention. Hence, the gold used is not just for decoration; it represents divine energy and power. This makes Tanjore art look royal, sacred, and distinct from other folk art styles.

How does one identify a Tanjore artwork?

- One main figure placed in the centre
- Shiny gold areas that catch the light
- Raised designs on jewellery, crowns, and clothes
- Bright colours like red, green, blue, and gold
- Decorative arches and borders around the figure

What makes it special?

Tanjore painting is different from any other Indian art form because it uses real gold foil and thick layers to create a raised surface. This makes the painting look 3-dimensional and glowing. The artwork focuses on gods, devotion, and richness rather than daily life or stories.

FACT FILES

- The gold in Tanjore paintings shines brighter when light falls on it.
- Some older Tanjore paintings used small stones to decorate jewellery.
- Most figures face forward to convey a strong and powerful presence.

ACTIVITY

BECOME A ROYAL DESIGNER!

Design only the frame, arch, and background that surrounds a Tanjore painting, NOT the main figure. Use patterns and shapes to make it look rich, ornate, and sacred.

PHAD ART | Scrolls of Tales

Type of Art Form

Phad painting is a traditional scroll painting made on long pieces of cloth. Unlike regular paintings, it is not meant to be viewed all at once. The scroll is unrolled slowly so the story can be followed scene by scene.

Place of Origin

Phad painting originated in Rajasthan, India. It developed in the desert regions where storytelling and oral traditions were critical to passing down history and culture.

Purpose of the Paintings

Phad paintings were made to tell stories visually. They were not created merely for decoration, but to help people understand and remember long stories through illustrations.

Phad paintings were used by travelling storytellers called Bhopas. They carried the scroll from village to village and performed stories before a live audience, usually at night.

Stories Depicted

The paintings often show stories of local heroes, gods, and warriors. Many moments from a story are shown together in one scroll, allowing the entire story to be told in a single artwork. The story is understood by looking at the pictures while listening to the storyteller, who explains each scene as the scroll is unrolled.

Visual Style

Figures in Phad painting are drawn flat and usually shown from the side. Bright colours are used, and the background is fully filled with figures and details, leaving no empty space.

Materials Used

Traditionally, Phad paintings are made on cloth using natural colours. This makes the scroll strong enough to be carried, folded, and reused many times.

What makes Phad different from other art forms?

Phad painting is special because it is meant to be performed, not merely viewed. The artwork, music, and storytelling join forces to make the painting feel alive rather than static.

ACTIVITY

Look at one section of a Phad painting. Imagine it being performed, and write the following:

ONE SOUND YOU MIGHT HEAR

ONE ACTION TAKING PLACE

ONE EMOTION DEPICTED IN THE SCENE

RANGOLI ART | Art that lives for a day

What is a Rangoli?

Rangoli is a traditional Indian floor art made by creating patterns on the ground. It is usually drawn at entrances using coloured powders, rice flour, flower petals, or sand. It is temporary and meant to be enjoyed for a short time.

Where did it originate?

Rangoli has been practised across India for centuries. It goes by different names across states, but the idea of welcoming positivity stays the same.

When and where is Rangoli used?

Rangoli is commonly made during festivals like Diwali, Pongal, Onam, and Navratri.
It is also used for weddings and ceremonies, usually near doorways, courtyards, and temples.

What do Rangoli designs depict?

Rangoli designs include geometric shapes, flowers, diyas, and traditional symbols. Many are symmetrical and balanced. Some are simple, while others are very detailed.

What materials are used to make Rangoli?

Traditionally, Rangoli was made using rice flour. Today, people also use coloured powders, chalk, sand, and flower petals. These materials are simple and easy to use.

How is Rangoli made?

Many Rangoli designs begin with small dots placed on the floor. These dots act as guides and are joined together using lines, curves, and patterns. Some Rangolis are drawn freehand, while others follow set designs passed down through families.

Why is Rangoli important?

Rangoli is believed to usher in good luck, happiness, and prosperity. It is also a way to welcome guests and mark special days with colour and creativity.

What makes Rangoli special?

Rangoli is unique because it is temporary. Once the day is over, the artwork disappears. This shows that art does not have to last forever to be meaningful.

Did you notice?

Rangoli designs usually grow from the centre outward, which helps keep the design balanced and even.

FUN FACTS

- Rangoli is made on the floor, not on paper or canvas.
- Many Rangoli designs start with dots before the lines are added and the colours filled in.
- Even the same Rangoli pattern never looks exactly the same twice.

ACTIVITY | COLOUR IN THE DESIGN

ACTIVITY | COLOUR IN THE DESIGN

ACTIVITY | COLOUR IN THE DESIGN

ACTIVITY

Using what you've read about Rangoli, create your own Rangoli design. Begin from the centre and develop your pattern outward with repeating shapes and balanced symmetry. Make your design colourful, festive, and inviting.

ROGAN ART | Precision on Fabric

An art that lives on fabric

Rogan art is a traditional Indian art form created directly on cloth. Instead of using brushes, artists draw designs using a thick, paste-like paint that sits raised on the fabric. This gives Rogan art a textured, glossy appearance with a distinct tactile feel.

A tradition from Kutch

The art form originated in the Kutch region of Gujarat. Rogan art is extremely rare and has been practised by only a few families for generations. The knowledge and technique are carefully passed down, making it a protected and valuable tradition.

How is the paint used?

The paint used in Rogan art is made from castor oil mixed with natural colours. It is applied using a metal rod or pointed tool. Artists guide the paint carefully, often without touching the cloth directly, which requires great control and steady hand movements.

Balance and Symmetry

Many Rogan designs are made by folding the cloth in half while the paint is still wet. When the cloth is opened, the design appears on both sides in perfect balance. This folding method creates symmetry that is difficult to achieve by hand.

What do the designs depict?

Rogan art usually features floral patterns, leaves, vines, and the famous "Tree of Life" motif. Designs often begin at the centre and slowly spread outward, filling the space in a calm and organised way.

Why makes Rogan art so special?

Rogan art stands out because of its combination of soft fabric and raised paint. The slow process, careful technique, and rare practice make each piece feel detailed, precious, and unique.

ACTIVITY

Draw a simple pattern on one side of a centre line. Carefully mirror the same pattern on the other side to make both sides look balanced and equal, inspired by the symmetry seen in Rogan art.

BLOCK PRINTING | Crafted One Press at a Time

What is Block Printing?

Block printing is a traditional Indian textile art where hand-carved wooden blocks dipped in dye are pressed onto fabric to create patterns.

The Origin Story

Block printing has been practised in India for centuries, especially in Rajasthan and Gujarat, where different regions developed their own styles and patterns.

Where do you see Block Printing today?

Today, block printing is seen on clothing items like sarees and kurtas, and home items such as bedsheets, curtains, and cushion covers.

How are the blocks made?

First, the wood: A strong piece of wood is chosen so the block can be used again and again.

Sketch the design: The pattern is drawn on the wood with coloured chalk.

Carve it out: The extra wood is carefully carved away so the design emerges.

Smooth the surface: Sharp or rough bits are cleaned so the print emerges well.

Add a handle: A small handle is fixed on the back to make printing easier.

Try a test print: The block is pressed onto scrap fabric to see how the design looks.

More colours, more blocks: If the design has many colours, a new block is made for each one.

ACTIVITY

Design your own block. From the steps above, we can see that choosing a design and creating the block are essential. If you were to use block printing on items for yourself, what design would you want printed?

www.ingramcontent.com/pod-product-compliance
Lightning Source LLC
LaVergne TN
LVHW070937210926
848482LV00003B/264
* 9 7 9 8 9 0 5 4 0 9 6 3 9 *